A miraculous
properties known across the world

●

Dr. Rajeev Sharma

MANOJ PUBLICATIONS

© *All Rights Reserved*

Publishers :

Manoj Publications
761, Main Road, Burari, Delhi-110084
Ph: 27611116, 27611349, Fax: 27611546
Mobile: 9868112194
E-mail: *info@manojpublications.com*
(For online shopping visit our website)
Website: *www.manojpublications.com*

Showroom :

Manoj Publications
1583-84, Dariba Kalan, Chandni Chowk
Delhi-110006
Ph.: 23262174, 23268216, Mob.: 9818753569

ISBN: 978-81-310-0742-6

Seventh Edition : 2014

Printers :
Jai Maya Offset
Jhilmil Industrial Area, Delhi-110095

BASIL : *Dr. Rajeev Sharma*

PREFACE

Tulsi (Basil) has diverse healing properties. Though traditionally used by Hindus now others are using it too recognizing its immense therapeutic properties. The Tulsi has the property of acting as an adaptogen. It balances different processes in the body and is of great help in stress management.

The extracts of tulsi have been used in traditional Indian Ayurvedic system of medicine. It is also used in the Unani system of medicine. Ayurvedic remedies for common colds, headaches, stomach disorders, inflammation, infections, heart disease, poisoning, cataracts and malaria make use of the tulsi. The tulsi acts on the nervous system and strengthens it. It strengthens the heart. It acts as an appetizer and promotes digestion too. It facilitates the secretion of digestive enzymes and prevents flatulence. Having detoxifying properties the tulsi purifies blood of any toxins that might be present in it.

Studies have also shown the tulsi to be effective in reducing blood sugar levels and in controlling diabetes. It has also been proved to be effective in reducing cholesterol levels. Having anti bacterial and anti parasitic properties makes it suitable for combating infectious diseases of various types. Recent findings have indicated that the tulsi may well provide protection from radiation poisoning. It has also been indicated that tulsi possesses anti cancerous properties. There has come up a belief that a tulsi leaf swallowed daily will ensure protection from cancer.

In this book the subject is covered to its full. We try our best to cover every aspect of Tulsi (Basil), its medicinal and industrial use along with home remedies.

—*Publishers*

CONTENTS

INTRODUCTION

It is known as Holy Basil in English and Tulsi in Sanskrit. Other names used for the Tulsi are Manjari, Krishna tulsi, Trittavu, Tulshi and Thulsi.

Description

Tulsi is a heavy branched having hair all over. It attains the height of about 75– 90 cm. It has round oval shaped leaves which are up to 5 cm long. The leaves are 2-4 cm in length. Its seeds are flat. Its flowers are purple–creamish in colour. The tulsi with the green leaves is called the Shri Tulsi and one with the reddish leaves is called the Krishna tulsi. Its seeds are yellow to reddish in colour. Leaves of Tulsi contains very essential oil. Tulsi is widely grown throughout India.

Cultivation Methods

Tulsi seeds germinate easily. The seeds are mainly sown in the spring season. They are watered from time to time and germinated in one to two weeks. Tulsi prefers rich soil for its growth. It requires full sunlight. It is mainly grown in the temperate climate.

Medicinal Uses

Tulsi has got the great medicinal value. Tulsi is taken as the herbal tea. The oil extracted from the karpoora tulsi is mostly used in the herbal toiletry. Its oil is also used against the insects and bacteria. The Rama tulsi is the effective remedy for the severe acute respiratory syndrome. Juice of its leaves gives relief in cold, fever, bronchitis and cough. Tulsi oil is also used as the ear drop. Tulsi helps in curing malaria. It is very effective against indigestion, headache, hysteria, insomnia and cholera. The fresh leaves of tulsi are taken by the million of people everyday. For over the centuries tulsi has been known for its remarkable healing properties.

Other Uses

Many people wears the tulsi beads, which is said to have certain physical and medicinal properties. Its wood is considered as more powerful than any other gem that helps in protecting one from the negative influences. One can also buy several handicraft jewellery items made of tulsi wood.

Cultural Importance

Tulsi is the sacred plant dearer to the Lord Vishnu. Tulsi symbolises purity. It is considered as the holy plant in the Indian subcontinent. Tulsi got its name from Tulasi Devi, who was one of Lord Krishna's eternal consorts. In India people grow tulsi as the religious plant and worship it. Its leaves are used in temples for the worship purposes and also on the several occasions such as marriage. A Hindu house is considered incomplete without the Tulsi plant in the courtyard. Tulsi is belived to promote longevity and life long happiness. Hindus perform special Tulsi Pooja in the Kartik month which starts after Sharad Poornima. It is the time of the Tulsi Vivah (marriage). On this day Tulsi is decorated and coloured as a bride.Even today people in India maintain a potted tulsi plant. The womens water the plant, light up the diya near it and worships it daily. The stems, leaves, seeds and even the soil is considered as holy. According to the ancient texts tulsi is glorified as the one who helps in bringing people closer to the divine.

□□

PROPERTIES OF TULSI

Tulsi is native to India, where it often graces shrines and homes as an aromatic perennial shrub. Tulsi is grown as an annual herb in temperate climates. The tulsi plant is pleasing to the eye, with an upright, open and branching form. The fragrance of the leaves is also quite attractive-spicy and complex, often resembling clove. The taste is excellent, especially when the dried leaves are brewed into tea. The flowers of purple or blue occur on multiple upright.

Types of Tulsi

Three main forms are generally recognized: Rama tulsi with stems and leaves of green, Krishna tulsi with stems and sometimes also leaves of purple, and Vana tulsi,

which is unmodified from its wild form. Tulsi exhibits great variation across its range and among the several domesticated cultivars. Variations in soil type and rainfall may also equate to a difference in the size and form of the plants as well as their medicinal strength and efficacy.

Cultivation of Tulsi from Seed

Tulsi seed is easy to germinate and grow. Sow the small tulsi seeds in early spring indoors or in the greenhouse for an early start, or sow tulsi seed directly in the spring or summer garden. Sow tulsi seeds just under the surface of the soil and press in firmly. Keep tulsi seed watered and warm until germination, which occurs within 1 to 2 weeks. Tulsi prefers full sun, rich soil, and plenty of water. Thin or transplant to 1 to 2 feet apart. Tulsi does well in pots or window boxes, and is traditionally grown for good luck near the front door of the house.

Traditional Uses

The uses of this plant are legion, and it is often taken in combination with other herbs. The fragrant leaves and flowers, in the form of tincture, tea or decoction are

considered to be stomachic and expectorant, used in treating coughs, bronchitis, skin diseases, and diarrhoea. These preparations are considered to be prophyllactic against epidemics including cholera, influenza and malaria. The tulsi seeds, taken mixed in water, juice or cow's milk, are antioxidant, nourishing, mucilagenous and demulcent. They are used in treating low energy, ulcers, vomiting and diarrhoea, or as an overall tonic. The powder of the dried root, taken in milk, ghee, or as a decoction, is recommended to treat malarial fever, as an analgesic application to the bites and stings of insects, and also to increase sexual stamina and prevent premature ejaculation.

Contemporary Uses

Tulsi is an uplifting and energy-enhancing adaptogenic herb, having much in common with other triterpenoid containing plants such as ginseng. The herb improves resistance to stress and has a normalizing influence on blood pressure and blood sugar imbalances. Used on a regular basis as tea, tulsi is likely to prove prophyllactic against the negative effects of environmental toxins, including cancer. The plant is also richly endowed with bioavailable antioxidants, vitamins A and C, and calcium.

❏❏

BENEFITS OF TULSI

Tulsi is the most worshipped plant in Hindu culture. It has a mythological background as tulsi is considered as Lord Krishna's wife. Literal meaning of tulsi is incomparable so as the name suggest, it really has properties that are incomparable with any other herb. Every thing mentioned in Indian mythology has a scientific background. So as the culture of planting tulsi in centre of courtyard in Hindu homes. It is a strong belief that those who plant tulsi in there houses never get ill, as it is very lovable to Lord Krishna and he has blessed this herb with this property. Scientific reason of this story is that tulsi contains such a chemical composition that no mosquitoes and flies can come near the plant because of it s peculiar odour. Thereby by planting tulsi in courtyard prevents entry of these creatures in house thus rendering home safe from any diseases caused by these organisms.

Biological name of tulsi is Ocimum sanctum and in common English language it is called holy basil. This herb is commonly found everywhere in India. Plant height varies from 2-4 ft. It flowers in winter season *i.e.* about December to February. It contains some biological active chemical compounds like ursolic acid, luteolin and apigenin extracted from leaves. Herb has *katu* and *tickta* rasa predominance. It is *ushna* (hot) *virya* in potency. It has *laghu* (light) and *ruksha* (dry) properties. Its major act is of as *krimighan* (anti bacterial and anti parasitic). Plant parts used are leaves, flower, seeds and root.

Tulsi is being used in variety of herbal ayurvedic formulations. Most dominantly it is used in bronchitis and asthmatic conditions. It gives great relief in cough especially one predominated by *kapha.*

Tulsi because of its great healing property has been indicated in variety of diseases. Being *ushna* (hot) in potency it is regarded as *vata* and *kapha* suppressant, hence all the diseases caused by vata and kapha can be treated with the help of tulsi.

As we begin with the skin problems, as mentioned earlier it acts as anti bacterial and anti parasitic, therefore is widely used in infectious diseases. It act on nervous system providing them strength, relieves stress and also helps in relieving pain, as it is vata suppressant. It work as appetizer and promotes digestion by helping in secretion of digestive enzymes. It helps in preventing flatulence and avoids constipated stool. It also keeps check on any infection that might invade our digestive system. Tulsi is also seen very useful in heart disease. It provides strength to heart and helps in proper working. It also helps to detoxify any toxin that might be circulating through our body via blood thereby have the property to purify blood.

Tulsi finds great importance in respiratory tract disease. It gives marvellous results in upper respiratory tract infection. As mentioned earlier that it acts rigorously on *kapha* hence it works as good expectorant relieving from wet cough. It also finds its good use in bronchitis and asthmatic conditions. It helps to fight the cause of allergy by which our respiratory tract gets inflamed and then resolves the causative agent. Good results have also been seen in anti-tubercular treatment as it works as antibiotic eliminating the bacteria. It also shows good results in chest pains. Tulsi finds great use in fever as it act as antipyretic, pain reliever, and provides strength to our body.

Some beneficial results were also seen in diabetes and micturation related problems. It also acts as an antidote for many poisons. Tulsi is known to possess anti-cancerous properties.

⬜⬜

TULSI—FULL OF WONDERS

Since time immemorial, Tuisi is not only renowned but also praised for its health promoting and disease preventing properties. Tulsi the sacred basil has captivated the imagination of man, from before the times of *Rigveda* for its good health and environmental benefits.

Tulsi is the plant that has made important costribution to the field of science from ancient times as also to modern research due to its large number of medicinal properties. Tulsi is one herb that possesses the anti-stress, anti-bacterial, anti viral, anti fungal, anti protozoal, anti oxidant and anti carcinogenic properties.

As sacred as Rama and Shyama, third type, of tulsi, the 'Van Tulsi' is termed as the 'very grateful basil.' Though the knowledge of this type of Tulsi variety is constrained, it can be used in the same manner as Rama and Shyama. Himalayas is the place where the Van Tulsi is mainly found but they are found in large abundance in North India.

Though with time, a number of herbal medicines have developed, the role of Tulsi cannot be ignored since it has played an important role in maintaining its doctrine and value in every household. Chemically, tulsi contains alkaloids, carbohydrates, proteins glycosides, phenols, spooning, tannins and terrene.

Consumption of tulsi in its raw form is more effective as, then, instead of providing selective ingredients, it provides us with its entire constitution. The *Padma Puran* and *Tulsi Kavacham* describe tulsi as a protector of life accompanying the human being form birth till death.

Even in faults that according to Ayurveda have *vatta*, *pitta and kapha*, literally meaning 'wind, bile and phlegm', Tulsi plays a very important role, as Ayurveda looks at disease with a holistic views-point and disturbance of normal physiological functions of the body.

Tulsi contains multiple bioactive substances as well as minerals and vitamins, normalizing the disturbed physiological functions of the body by harmonizing the different imbalance that is confirmed with the an dent Ayurvedic concepts of *Tridoshas.*

Tulsi possesses anti- stress or adaptogenic properties having a staminator effect. The extracts of Tulsi leaf also helps in inhibiting the enzyme of filarial worm, anti-tubercular, anti-funngal, anti-viral function as it possess the hypo-choloestromic activity.

The most dreaded disease AIDS can also be regulated with its anti-AIDS properties. Tulsi is useful In AIDS and it markedly reduces cell-mediated immunity. Tulsi also affects the central nervous system by prolonging the time of lost reflex.

Not only this, ancient texts like *Sushruta Samhita, Padma Puran* and *Garuda Puran*, after centuries of observation in humans, also describes tulsi as a 'child giver' and great spermatogenic agent.

□□

TULSI—THE HOLY HEALER

Tulsi is an important symbol of the Hindu religious tradition. Although the word 'tulsi' gives the connotation of the incomparable one, its other name, Vishnupriya, means the one that pleases Lord Vishnu. Found in most of the Indian homes and worshipped, its legend has permeated Indian ethos down the ages. Tulsi has been adored in almost all ancient ayurvedic texts although for its extraordinary medicinal properties.

Known in English as Holy Basil, tulsi is pungent and bitter in taste and hot, light and dry in effect. Its seeds are considered to be cold in effect. It has been described as of two types—*vanya* (wild) and *gramya* (grown in homes). Although having identical usage, the former has darker leaves. Seeds, roots and leaves of the plant are medicinal.

Ayurvedic texts categorise Tulsi as stimulant, aromatic and antipyretic. While alleviating *kapha* and *vata*, it aggravates *pitta*. It has a wide range of action on the human body mainly as a cough alleviator, a sweat-inducer and a mitigator of indigestion and anorexia.

Tulsi also has antibacterial, anti-inflammatory, anthelmentic and blood-purifying properties. Extensive research has found it to be an anabolic, adaptogenic and immuno-modulator drug. Its anti-tubercular activity is one-tenth of the potency of streptomycin and one-fourth of that of isonizid.

Tulsi is a popular home remedy for a number of ailments. Here are a few tips:

Fever

Tulsi leaves are specific for many fevers. In the case of

malaria and of other tropical infections, a decoction of tulsi leaves boiled with powdered cardamom in a cup of water and strengthened with sugar and milk brings down the temperature. Tea prepared with a little of ginger and leaves of tulsi, while allaying bodyache, also gives a freshening feeling.

Respiratory Disorders

In bronchitis and asthma, Tulsi juice is used as a medium of the intake of the medicine. In acute cough and cold, taking half a teaspoonful of dried leaves of Tulsi and black pepper, added with a little of honey, works well. Tulsi is also an important ingredient of many Ayurvedic cough syrups.

Stress Management

Taking the lead from the recent studies that tulsi has stress-busting and antioxidant properties, more and more pharmaceutical companies are coming up with its preparations. However, a healthy person can take up to 10 leaves of Tulsi in a day.

Skin Diseases and Headache

Applied locally, Tulsi juice is beneficial in the treatment of ringworm and other minor skin diseases. Its pounded leaves, mixed with sandalwood paste, is a famous home remedy for headache. Tulsi seeds are used in anti-leucoderma preparations.

Other Diseases

A decoction of 10 to 20 leaves taken along with a pinch of rock salt abates digestive problems like flatulence and anorexia. Its seeds are given in chronic urinary infections and with their mucilagenous action they are also helpful in treating diarrhoea, habitual constipation and piles. The dose of tulsi juice is 10 to 20 ml whereas the seed powder can be taken from one to three gm twice a day.

□□

TULSI—THE POWER PLANT

The 'tulsi' plant is an important symbol in the Hindu religious tradition. The name 'tulsi' connotes 'the incomparable one'. Tulsi is a venerated plant and Hindus worship it in the morning and evening. Tulsi grows wild in the tropics and warm regions. Dark or Shyama tulsi and light or Rama tulsi are the two main varieties of basil, the former possessing greater medicinal value. Of the many varieties, the Krishna or Shyama tulsi is commonly used for worship.

The presence of tulsi plant symbolizes the religious bent of a Hindu family. A Hindu household is considered incomplete if it doesn't have a tulsi plant in the courtyard. Many families have the tulsi planted in a specially built structure, which has images of deities installed on all four sides, and an alcove for a small earthen oil lamp. Some households can even have up to a dozen tulsi plants on the verandah or in the garden forming a miniature basil forest.

The Holy Herb

Places that tend to inspire concentration and places ideal for worship, according to the *Gandharva Tantra*, include "grounds overgrown with tulsi plants". The Tulsi Manas Mandir at Varanasi is one such famous temple, where tulsi is worshipped along with other Hindu gods and goddesses. Vaishnavites or believers of Lord Vishnu worship the tulsi leaf because it's the one that pleases Lord Vishnu the most. They also wear beaded necklaces made of tulsi stems. The manufacture of these tulsi necklaces is a cottage industry in pilgrimages and temple towns.

An Elixir

Apart from its religious significance it is of great medicinal significance, and is a prime herb in Ayurvedic treatment. Marked by its strong aroma and a stringent taste, tusli is a kind of 'the elixir of life' as it promotes longevity. The plant's extracts can be used to prevent and cure many illnesses and common ailments like common cold, headaches, stomach disorders, inflammation, heart disease, various forms of poisoning and malaria. Essential oil extracted from karpoora tulsi is mostly used for medicinal purposes though of late it is used in the manufacture of herbal toiletry.

When Hindu women worship tulsi, they in effect pray for less and less carbonic acid and more and more oxygen—a perfect object lesson in sanitation, art and religion. The tulsi plant is even known to purify or de-pollute the atmosphere and also works as a repellent to mosquitoes, flies and other harmful insects. Tulsi used to be a universal remedy in cases of malarial fever.

Tulsi in Legends

Quite a few myths and legends found in the *Puranas* point to the origin of importance of tulsi in religious rituals. Although tulsi is regarded as feminine, in no folklore is she described as the consort the Lord. Yet a garland solely made of tulsi leaves is the first offering to the Lord as part of the daily ritual. The plant is accorded the sixth place among the eight objects of worship in the ritual of the consecration of the *Kalasha*, the container of holy water.

According to one legend, tulsi was the incarnation of a princess who fell in love with Lord Krishna, and so had a curse laid on her by his consort Radha. Tulsi is also mentioned in the stories of Meera and of Radha immortalised in Jayadev's *Gita Govinda*. The story of Lord Krishna has it that when Krishna was weighed in gold, not even all the ornaments of Satyabhama could outweigh him. But a single tulsi leaf placed by Rukmani on the pan tilted the scale.

In the Hindu mythology, tulsi is very dear to Lord Vishnu. Tulsi is ceremonially married to Lord Vishnu annually on the 11th bright day of the month of Kartika in the lunar calendar. This festival continues for five days and concludes on the full moon day, which falls in mid October. This ritual, called the 'Tulsi Vivah' inaugurates the annual marriage season in India.

□□

THE MEDICINAL PLANT

Holy Basil has many medicinal uses, including antibacterial and antiviral properties. It is helpful for coughs, upper respiratory infections, bronchitis, stress-related skin disorders and indigestion. An herb that has its own mythological background. Tulsi is supposed to be a beloved of Lord Krishna, a reincarnation of Lord Vishnu. This herb is worshipped throughout India as well as in various other parts of this world.

Tulsi inhibits inflammation causing enzymes in our bodies which contribute to arthritis pain and other kinds of inflammation. The anti-inflammatory effects of Tulsi are comparable to ibuprofen, naproxen and aspirin. Tulsi even enhances the adrenal function by lowering cortisol levels. This results in reducing the negative effects of stress. Tulsi extracts protect us against mercury toxicity. We build up mercury deposits in our system from eating fish and even inserting dental fillings. Tulsi helps extract this mercury from our body, thus purifying it. Tulsi has antimicrobial, anti-inflammatory, expectorant properties and is useful in respiratory tract infections. It helps during respiratory stress.

Fever & Common Cold

The leaves of basil are specific for many fevers. During the rainy season, when malaria and dengue fever are widely prevalent, tender leaves, boiled with tea, act as a preventive against these diseases. In case of acute fevers, a decoction of the leaves boiled with powdered cardamom in half a liter of water and mixed with sugar and milk to bring down the body temperature of the patient. The juice of tulsi leaves can be used to bring down fever. Extract of tulsi leaves in fresh water should be given every 2 to 3 hours.

Cough

Tulsi is an important constituent of many Ayurvedic cough syrups and expectorants. It helps to mobilize the mucus in bronchitis and asthma. Chewing tulsi leaves relieves cold and flu.

Sore Throat

Water boiled with tulsi leaves is taken as to drink in case of sore throat. This water can also be used for the purpose of gargles.

Respiratory Disorders

The herb is very useful in the treatment of respiratory system disorders. A decoction of the leaves, with honey and ginger is an effective remedy for bronchitis, asthma, influenza, cough and cold. For the immediate relief in the cases of influenza the decoction of the leaves, cloves and common salt is given for immediate relief.

Stress

Tulsi leaves are regarded as an 'adaptogen' or anti-stress agent. Recent studies have shown that the leaves provide its user with the significant protection against stress. Even healthy persons can chew 12 leaves of tulsi, twice a day, to prevent stress. It even purifies the blood and helps prevent several common disorders or ailments.

Improves Beta Cell Function

The leaves of the tulsi plant contain various essential oils within them. It is therefore very useful in improving pancreatic beta cell function and thus enhancing the insulin secretion to keep a check over the blood sugar within the patients suffering by diabetes.

Respiratory Tract Problems

Tulsi is very effective in treating the cold and related disorders. It is a boon for respiratory tract disorders. It helps in treating all the disorders, which are related to throat. It increases the immunity of the body therefore it helps in fighting against any antigen or infection that invades our body. It is also very helpful in expelling out the extra mucus that gets accumulated in our respiratory tract especially in lungs or the respiratory passages.

Headache

There are even certain analgesic properties in tulsi and are a great assert in providing remedy to various pains in the body. Tulsi is very helpful in relieving headaches. It contains certain compounds that helps to release the spasm in the muscles hence is extremely helpful in relaxing the body.

Abdominal Disorders

It is one of the potent herbs in treatment of all a kinds of abdominal disorders. It is very effective in increasing the peristaltic movements in the GI tract. It is very helpful in improving the appetite. It also has some mild laxative properties therefore helps in evacuation of the bowel and the maintenance of a healthy bowel.

Inflammation

Tulsi is considered a good herb with anti-inflammatory properties. It is very effective in suppressing any kind of edema that happening in the body. It is very much used in reducing the pain and improve the blood circulation in the body therefore is very helpful in dealing with any type of the swellings that are found to be occurring in our bodies.

Heart Diseases

Tulsi is useful in heart related problems. It gives strength to the heart muscles and also improves the blood circulation. It also helps in improving the blood supply to heart muscles. It is also helpful in reducing the cholesterol levels in the body.

Actions of Tulsi :

☐ Protects and reduces stress.

☐ Improves stamina and endurance.

☐ Boosts immune system.

☐ Diminishes symptoms of colds, coughs and flu.

☐ Reduces inflammation.

☐ Scavenges the free radicals and defies the aging factors.

☐ Powerful antioxidant.

☐ Antibiotic, antiviral and antifungal properties.

☐ Reduction of nausea, vomiting and cramping.

☐ Very effective in bringing down the temperature in many types of fevers.

☐ Supports the heart, lungs and liver.

☐ Helps in the maintenance of a healthy digestive system.

☐ As its improves the working capability of Beta

pancreatic cells so is very useful in blood-glucose management.

☐ Supports oral and periodontal health and maintains a normal oral hygiene.

☐ Encourages efficient use of oxygen.

☐ Protects against radiation damage.

☐ It acts as anti bacterial and anti parasitic, therefore is widely used in infectious diseases.

☐ Holy basil act on nervous system providing them strength, relieves stress and helps in relieving pain.

☐ It work as appetizer and promotes digestion by helping in secretion of digestive enzymes.

☐ Tulsi juice when mixed with ginger juice is very effective in abdominal disorder in children.

☐ It helps in preventing flatulence and avoids constipated stool.

☐ It is an effective natural cure for upper respiratory tract infection.

☐ Holy basil works as good expectorant relieving from wet cough.

☐ It is very useful in bronchitis and asthmatic conditions.

☐ It works as antibiotic eliminating the bacteria.

☐ It is widely used in fever as it act as antipyretic, pain reliever, and provides strength to our body. Take powder of holy basil leaves with saunth (dried ginger) and sugar with hot water in fevers.

☐ It also possesses anti-cancerous properties.

☐ Tulsi juice drops are very effective in earache.

☐ Keep powder of tulsi root in water for overnight and take it early morning for diabetes natural cure.

☐ It works as a powerful antioxidant thereby helps in preventing early aging signs and makes the skin young.

☐☐

IMPORTANCE AND INGREDIENTS OF TULSI

Tulsi is a Divine plant in India.The most sacred herbs of India are likely Tulsi and Lotus, and of these tulsi, no doubt, inspires the most personal devotion. Where most herbs are considered to be forms of the Goddess, Tulsi is a considered to be a Goddess herself.Tulsi is a very friendly herb and consistently lends herself well in all sorts of therapies.There are three types of Tulsi Plants,depending upon their colour of leaves—Rama, Krishna and Vana tulsi.

Tulsi is a widely grown, sacred plant of India. It is also called by names like Manjari/Krishna Tulsi (Sanskrit), Trittavu (Malayalam), Tulshi (Marathi) and Thulsi (Tamil

& Telegu). It is called Holy Basil in English. The natural habitat of Tulsi varies from sea level to an altitude of 2000m. It is found growing naturally in moist soil nearly all over the globe. In India, Hindus grow Tulsi as a religious plant in their homes, temples and their farms. They use Tulsi leaves in routine worship. This plant is also grown as a pot herd and in home gardens.

Tulsi is a branched, fragrant and erect herb having hair all over. It attains a height of about 75 to 90 cm when mature. Its leaves are nearly round and up to 5 cm long with the margin being entire or toothed. These are aromatic because of the presence of a kind of scented oil in them. A variety with green leaves is called Rama Tulsi and one with reddish leaves is called Krishna tulsi. Tulsi flowers are small having purple to reddish colour, present in small compact clusters on cylindrical spikes. The fruits are small and the seeds yellow to reddish in colour. Because of its medicinal virtues, Tulsi is used in Ayurvedic preparations for treating various ailments.

Tulsi leaves contain a bright yellow volatile oil which is useful against insects and bacteria. The oil is reported to possess anti-bacterial properties and acts as an insecticide. It has marked insecticidal activity against mosquitoes. The juice of leaves, and a concoction, called *jushanda*, a kind of tea, gives relief in common cold, fever, bronchitis, cough, digestive complaints, etc. When applied locally, it helps in eradicating ringworms and other skin diseases. Tulsi oil is also used as ear drops in case of pain. The seeds are used in curing urinary problems. Aphrodisiac virtue has been attributed to it, where powdered Tulsi root with clarified butter (ghee) is prescribed.

The medicinal effect of all the varieties is almost similar, if not the same. The best part of the matter is that certain Indian scientists are at the threshold of finalising their discovery of a reliable medicine against cancer out of Tulsi plant.

□□

GENERAL PROPERTIES OF TULSI

Tulsi is such a pious plant for almost all the people of the world that it is worshipped like a goddess. In the Hindus, no food is sacred enough to be offered to any god unless it has a few leaves of tulsi put on it. In fact, the sacred divine potion 'Panchamrita' has tulsi as one of the basic ingredients. Since it is full of the medicinal qualities, it is accorded this exalted status. In fact, all the religious rituals are borne out of some practical necessities. The ancients found tulsi to have great practical uses for health and hence they made it almost a divine plant.

Mythologically it is believed to have originated from the 'Great Churning of the Sea' performed by the Demons and Deities. Lord Vishnu is believed to be the most beloved god of this plant who is said to accept no offering of food unless some tulsi leaves are part of it. Since Lord Krishna is believed to be the incarnation of Lord Vishnu, he made tulsi widely grown in the Braj region. Vrindavan was believed to be a dense forest of tulsi plants. In Sanskrit one of the names of tulsi is Vrinda and hence Vrindavan means a thick forest of tulsi. The Ayurvedic treatises speak in superlative terms for this plant. They say that regular consumption of tulsi keeps palate, throat, teeth, gums, bronchal chord and lungs free of any sort of infection. That is why every house of the traditional Hindus has this plant. They say an invisible oil permeates itself from this plant in entire atmosphere and keeps it clean and free of germs. Even mere presence of tulsi is believed to have very salubrious effect on human body.

Another good quality of tulsi is its being antitoxic and hence anathema to all the poisonous insects and reptiles. If you have a tulsi plant in your garden or terrace, no snake and scorpion will come near it. That is why it is a religious ritual to keep a tulsi plant in every house or in the adjoining area. Not only the plant but also the soil in which it is planted becomes a very good tonic for health. That is why each and every part of this plant is believed to be sacred, medicinally and spiritually alike.

Another scientifically proved quality of tulsi is its being an insulatory material for electric impulses. It is believed that a house which has a tulsi plant cannot be subjected to the fall of lightning. This plant itself is full of electrical energy and its presence thus helps in the smooth circulation of blood. It is, perhaps, because of this reason that people wear small beads made of tulsi stalks over their heart region, hands and around the neck. If you wear such a Tulsi-lace around your waist you shall not be troubled by waist, liver, spleen or private parts' afflictions. Many Englishmen also started using a piece of tulsi wood in the Ninteenth Century in Calcutta to ward off such troubles.

Tulsi is not only sacred to the Hindus, even the Christians accord it an exalted status religiously. The Christian holy book says that this plant had sprouted up on its own over the grave of Christ. That is why the Churches of Eastern Europe still worship these leaves. Deeming them to be the gift of Christ and celebrate a Saint Basil's day on which the Christian ladies plant it in their orchards amidst a religious pageantry.

In fact tulsi has been found to be storehouse of virtues for the entire human system. Its leaves are very good medicines to cure a scores of disease, its blossom, rind and stalks keep your skin and muscles in good trim if used externally. Sometimes its blossom is dried and beads are made from it. They say if its dried blossom is rubbed over body, it provides an invisible effect to make body immune to all afflictions and illnesses.

Tulsi is a sacred plant almost all over the world. Whether you go to Israel or Mauritus or as far away as Indonesia, you would find its plant worshiped as though it is God.

The juice of tulsi is a recognised medicine in Homeopathic treatment. Not only Homeopaths, but physicians all over the world use it in one form or the other. Dr. Boerick of California opined in a science journal that tulsi juice was specially a good tonic for ladies. Its regular consumption protect them from all the feminine disorders. The declaration was made in the Imperial Malarial Conference held a few decades ago that alone Tulsi-leaves were capable of not only curing malaria but also in preventing its occurence. The oil of tulsi plant, when massaged over body cures even such dreadful diseases and affliction as paralysis or hemiflegia.

Tulsi has great preservative qualities. It is customary in far eastern islands to plant tulsi over their near and dears' graves. Perhaps they took a cue from this plant's emergence over Christ's grave. The scientific reason ascribed to this phenomenon is that the presence of tulsi prevents decay and again, taking a cue from Christ's Resurrection, as some Christians believe, the planters think that tulsi plant on the grave might revive the dead.

Moreover, if there be any decay or putrification of the body, the sweet smell of tulsi will overpower that foul smell.

Well, apart from the mythological factors, tulsi plant has innumerable virtues even scientifically. Its leaves have a rich quality of sulphur and doused lead combination which has its nectareous effect on the body. tulsi leaves keep the blood pressure on even keel, its consumption neither makes the person lecherous nor impotent; it helps him keep his sexual urge well within control. It saves from all the respiratory and digestive troubles and keeps the blood clean. It provides strength to the bones yet keep them supple. It leaves' juice is the best tonic for the skin.

Tulsi's actual growth period in India is from mid-July to mid-Nov. The traditional belief based on a botanical fact is that tulsi plant cannot survive the extreme heat and cold as it is very delicate. Hence in the traditional Hindu households, the 'Marriage of Tulsi' is solemnised with Lord Krishna on the bright Ekadashi of the Kartik month (first week of Nov.) and then a red cotton cloth is covered over it, apparently to signify its marriedhood but inherently to preserve it from the extreme cold and extreme heat. Its plant grow about two to three feet high and remains verdant if properly looked after.

⬜⬜

MEDICINAL EFFECTS OF TULSI

Tulsi is ubiquitous in Hindu tradition. Perhaps its role as a healing herb was instrumental in its 'sacred' implication. Tulsi is perhaps the most common and most revered of all household plants in India.

Tulsi is an erect sweet-scented herb, 30-100cm in height, growing in abundance near cultivated field gardens and waste lands. Its leaves, seeds ands whole plant is useful.

Ayurvedic practice recommends tulsi in several formulations to enhance immunity and metabolic functions as well as in the management of respiratory problems.

Chemical Constituents

A variety of biologically active compounds have been isolated from the leaves including ursolic acid, apigenin and luteolin.

Pharmacological Effects

In traditional Ayurvedic system of medicine, several medicinal properties have been attributed to this plant.

Recent pharmacological studies have established the anabolic, hypoglycemic, smooth muscle relaxant, cardiac depressant, antifertility, adaptogenic and immuno-modulator properties of this plant.

Antimicrobial Effects

Essential oil of tulsi have antibacterial, antifungal and antiviral properties. Its antitubercular activity is one-tenth the potency of streptomycin and one-fourth that of isoniazid.

Preperations containing tulsi extract significantly shorten the course of illness, clinical symptoms and the biochemical parameters in patients with viral hepatitis and viral encephalitis.

Antimalarial Effects

Essential oil of tulsi has been reported to possess 100 percent larvicidal activity against the mosquitoes. Trials have shown excellent antimalarial activity of tulsi. Its extracts have marked insecticidal activity against mosquitoes. Its repellant action lasts for about two hours.

Antiallergic and Immunomodulator Effects

Essential oil of Tulsi was found to have anti allergic properties. When administered to laboratory animals, the compound was found to inhibit mast cell degranulation and histamine release in the presence of allergen. These studies reveal the potential role of extracts in the management of immunological disorders including allergies and asthma.

Antifertility Effect

One of the major constituents of the leaves, ursolic acid has been reported to possess antifertility activity in rats and mice. This effect has been attributed to it's antiestrogenic effect which may be responsible for arrest of spermatogenesis in males and inhibitory effecton implantation of ovum in females. This constituent may prove to be a promising antifertility agent devoid of side effects.

Antidiabetic Effect

A randomized, placebo-controlled cross-over single blind trial on 40 human volunteers suffering from Type II diabetes was performed. During the four week trial, subjects alternately received a daily dose of 2.5 grams of tulsi leaves powder for two week periods. The results showed 17.6 percent reduction in fasting blood glucose and 7.3 percent decline in postprandial blood glucose on treatment with Tulsi as compared to the blood glucose levels during treatment with placebo.

For Heart Ailments

As Tulsi has a positive effect over blood pressure and also a de-toxicant, its regular use prevents heart attacks. A tonic may be prepared by mixing 1 gm of dry tulsi leaves with a spoonful of butter and some candy sugar or honey.Take twice a day; first thing in the morning and before going to bed at night. The drinking of tulsi-leaves tea keeps the blood pressure even.

Other Effects

The leaves in the form of a paste are used in parasitical diseases of the skin and also applied to the finger and toe nails during fever when the limbs are cold. The juice of the leaves is given in catarrh and bronchitis in children. The plant is said to have carminative, diaphoretic and stimulant properties. A decoction of the plant is used for cough and also as mouth wash for relieving tooth ache. It is good for headache, convulsions, cramps, fevers and cholera.

The drinking of tulsi-leaves tea keeps one free from cough and colds and other ailments associated with *kapha dosha* in the body.

This tea is an instant pick-me-up (energy drink) also.

□□

USES IN DIFFERENT DISEASES

God gifted tulsi plant has several medicinal properties for different ailments.

Cold and Cough

The chronic patient of this problem have their hair going untimely grey. To stop the process and cure it, take 300 gms. of tulsi leaves dried in shade, 50 gms. of Dalchini, 100 gms. tejpat, 200 gms. saunf (aniseeds), 200 gms. of small cardamom, agiya 300 gms; banfshaw 25 gms; red sandal 200 gms. and brahmi herb 200 gms. Grind all these ingredients and strain them through a cloth. Now take 10 gms. of this powder, boil it in 500 ml. water and when just a cup of this water remains, add sugar and milk and drink it twice a day like you have tea. All these problems will vanish in a couple of days.

Dirty Water-purifying Agent

Sometimes people don't like water of a new place. Just put a couple of Tulsi leaves and then you'd face no problem. If you put just two leaves of tulsi in a pitcher of water for an hour or so, and then remove them, the water shall be purified immediately.

Ear-pain

Take about 10 leaves of makoy and the leaves of tulsi. Extract their juice together and put it in the affected ear when it is slightly lukewarm (heat it a little in the sun). Alternatively add half a tablet of camphor in tulsi juice and put this juice in the ear for instant relief.

Eye Troubles

Put a drop of tulsi juice mixed with even quantity of honey for all sort of eye troubles, especially pain and burning. This solution can also be preserved in a bottle. In the problem of trachoma, grind ten leaves of tulsi together with a clove. Put it into your eyes every four hours. If swelling also persist in the eyes, add a little of tulsi juice with alum and apply in eyes for instant relief.

Epilepsy

Rub tulsi juice over body every day after taking bath. Keep the blossoms of tulsi inside the fold of hanky every time. At the time of attack, smell the blossom deeply. Should the attack make one unconscious, grind 11 leaves of tulsi, add a little salt to it and put a few drops of this juice in the patient's nostrils. He would immediately regain his consciousness. Keep a tulsi plant in verandah or somewhere near bed room.

Flatulence

Take about 10 gms. of tulsi juice, 10 gms. of dry ginger and 20 gms. of jaggery. Mix all of them together to form small tablets. Take this tablet thrice a day with water to set right your digestive process. But during the period you have this trouble, better keep fast or take only easily digestible food.

Fistula

Have three or four tulsi leaves every morning with water. Alternatively take the root of tulsi plant and the fruit of neem tree (Nimboli) and grind togther. Take 2 gms. of this combination every morning with whey for quick relief.

Flu

Take about 10 gms. of tulsi leaves and 250 ml. of water.

34

Boil them together till water is halved. Now add and the remaining water-rock salt according to taste. No sooner did you start to sweat the effect of flu shall be removed with the sweat and you shall be alright. Alternatively drink decoction of tulsi leaves, black pepper and batasha for more quicker relief.

Hoarse Voice

Just extract the juice of 10 tulsi leaves, add a little of honey and lick it. Just a small spoonful quantity of this solution will soothen your throat nerves and your voice will be again sweet.

Hair Trouble

Put about 21 leaves of tulsi and 10 gms. of amla powder in a big bowl. Add a little of water to make a paste of it. Apply it evenly on head and allow it to dry. Then wash it with cold water. This will prevent hair loss and clear dandruff also.

Heart Troubles

Tulsi is very effective to cure all sort of heart troubles. Since it controls blood pressure and keeps blood clean, its regular consumption prevents heart attacks. For especial tonic for heart, prepare the medicine in the following way. Take about 1 gm. dried powder of Arjun tree and mix even amount of honey. Now either churn or mix them till the solution is fully homogenous. Take about 1 gm. of this paste, add a little more of honey and lick it at least thrice a day, preferably early in the morning as the first thing, an hour after lunch and as the last thing before retiring for the day.

Hysteria

If the hysteric effect is due to excess of phlegm in the body, make the patient smell tulsi leaves and drink five tulsi leaves juice. If it is caused by the excessive heat going to the head, grind five tulsi leaves and five black pepper by mixing them in water and make the patient drink this water every morning and evening for a week's time. The hysteria will be cured.

Indigestion

Take the seeds of tulsi and peepal in equal quantity and grind them to fine powder form. Now add 3 gms. of this powder with a spoonful of honey and lick it twice a day to clear indigestion.

Drinking the tea of tulsi leaves also brings quick relief. The filthy substance will get out of the body with sweat and urine. Alternatively add 1gm. of rock salt in 10 gms. of tulsi leaves paste and swallow it down with water.

Insomnia

The easiest and best treatment of this problem is to pluck 51 leaves of tulsi. Give just one leaf to patient to chew and spread rest of the leaves evenly below his pillow and the corners of bed below the bed sheet. As the smell of tulsi leaves strikes his nostril, the pereson will feel sleepy and soon he will fall into sleep.

Itching

Extract juice of tulsi and massage on the parts of the body itching. If the trouble is chronic, take about 2 parts of tulsi juice and one part of til oil. Allow them to parboil on low fleme. Then cool it and put it in a bottle. This is a most effective oil for all sorts of itching problems.

Jaundice

Add 10 gms. tulsi leaves' juice in about 50 ml. of radish juice. Add a little of jaggery to the combination to sweeten it. Have this solution twice or thrice daily for about a month for getting total relief from this problem.

Alternatively take 3 gms. of tulsi leaves juice and 3 gms. of the root of punarnava. Mix them both in 50 ml. of water and drink it for about 15 days. This is a very effective dose to cure jaundice.

Kidney Troubles

For any type of kidney trouble, tulsi juice provides a very effective cure. Just soak 5 to 7 gms. of tulsi seeds overnight in water. In the morning grind them with sugar and drink the combination. Soon the congestion or infection in kidney will be thrown out by means of copious discharge of urine.

Leprosy

Living in an atmosphere abounding with tulsi plants is the best treatment. For white patches chew 5 leaves of tulsi every morning, evening and afternoon. Licking the combination of tulsi leaves juice with honey will cure the trouble quickly.

Leucoderma

Grind 10 gms. tulsi leaves with a clove of garlic and apply the paste on the affected portion every day, use this for 10 days for total relief.

Lethargy

The tea made of tulsi leaves provides instant energy and makes one quite energetic. This is not a cumbersome preposition because as you prepare tea, so you prepare this tulsi tea and instead of putting tea leaves, put tulsi leaves. The regular intake of this tea shall not only provide energy but will also keep you away from all the diseases borne out of the vitiation of kapha (phlegm) in the body.

Migraine

Get a small bunch of tulsi blossom; dry it in the shade and grind it to powder form. Just take two gms. of it, mix about half a spoonful of honey to it and make the person lick it. God willing, you may never require second dose, for it is a very efficacious treatment. In case you feel like, have another dose by the evening for a total cure.

Mouth-boils

Take just a leaf of chameli plant, and four leaves of tulsi. Chew them properly for a few minutes and suck in the juice. In about a day the trouble will vanish.

Malaria

Take about 10 gms. of tulsi leaves juice and add to it 1 gm. of ground black pepper. Administer this dose five or six days after every two hours. Alternatively make small tablets of this combination and feed the patient on tulsi tea additionally. In a couple of days the fever will vanish alongwith the malarial infection.

Night Blindness

Put two drops of tulsi leaves every morning and evening and drink the juice also at three times a day. Continue the treatment for about a month time for total cure.

Black pepper is also very effective to cure this trouble.

Put some black pepper grains in a wet cloth to allow them to bloat up. Now remove their rinds and grind them in tulsi juice. Line this paste in your eyes every morning and evening for total cure.

Nose-bleeding

The easiest and most effective cure of this trouble is to keep the tulsi blossom near you and smell it as and when you like. For those who are chronic patient of this trouble, this simple treatment is very effective and cures the trouble almost totally. Drinking tulsi juice mixed with honey will also help and provide extra strength to the body.

Paralysis

Boil a few leaves of tulsi in a tumblerful of water. When cool, strain and put this water in a bottle. Massage this water on the affected limbs. Continue this treatment for at least two weeks. This treatment, coupled with regular intake of the tulsi leaves will produce the desired results.

Pneumonia

Get the pure tulsi oil from a recognised Ayurvedic medicine shop. Put this oil on the chest of the afflicted person. Together with this treatment, extract the juice of five tulsi leaves, mix with it a few ground grains of black pepper at 6 hourly intervel. This combined treatment will produce enough heat in the body to make the person sweat. With sweat all the effect of cold inside the body shall vanish and the patient will be cured.

Chicken Pox

If the person already afflicted with this problem, then giving tulsi leaves juice mixed with ajwain (Bishop's weeds) will provide relief. But to prevent this menace afflicting you or your family members, prepare anti chicken pox tablets in the following way and administer one tablet daily with water.

Take 5 gms. tulsi leaves, 2.5 gms. javitri,1/2 gm. real pearl ash, 20 grains black pepper, 1/2 gm. saffron and 1/4 gm. cloves. Add water to make these tablets.

Spleen Enlargement

Take 5 gms. tulsi leaves dried under shade, 5 gms. indra jav and grind both of them to powder form. Add a little of salt and take the combination with a glass of cold water. Continue this treatment every morning and evening for 10 to 15 days. The effect of tulsi leaves will bring spleen to size and cure the trouble.

Sluggish Liver

Take five tulsi leaves, 2 gms. roasted powder of cumin seeds and 2 gms. of black salt. Grind them together to make it come in a homogenous powder form. Add to it even amount of the kernal of the wood-apple. Mix the combination in about 100 gms. of curd to reactivate the sluggish liver. For early relief from any sort of stomach disorder, drink a spoonful of the combination of the juices of the tulsi and ginger.

Stones

Make the patient sit on a chair having a commode like opening on the seat. Now prepare the decoction of the blossoms of tulsi, *i.e.* boil about 100 gms. of tulsi blossom in a litre of water. When the vapours start emerging, bring the container and stove beneath the chair on which the patient is seated. The moment the vapour starts touching the private organ, it would dissolve the stone. Continue this treatment for about a week for total cure.

T.B.

Grind together five grains of black pepper and five leaves of tulsi. Then mix the combination with half a spoonful of honey and lick it. Make the patient lick this combination twice daily. In winter season, add a little of ginger juice, the husk of wheat and a little of salt also in the combination.This is a very effective treatment but it has to continue quite long. Externally, rubbing a little of tulsi juice and ginger juice's mixture over the lungs shall bring the desired relief. Continue the treatment for about two months. Continue antitubercular treatment too.

Testes Problem

If there is swelling on the testes or any other problem concerning with testes, apply the paste prepared in the following manner over the testes. Take about 5 gms. each of a camel's dung, *amarbel* (easily available in Mango groves), the leaves of *arhar* and tulsi-leaves. Grind them to a homogenous paste in a little of cow's urine. When the paste is ready, apply it over the testes thickly. Allow it to dry and remove it in the morning. A week's treatment will cure all troubles connected with the testes.

Urinary Problems

For any sort of this trouble, soak about 5 to 7 gms. of tulsi seeds overnight in water. In the morning grind these seeds in water, add a litttle of sugar to the combination to make it more tasty. Drink this combination early in the morning and also in the afternoon, *i.e.* twice a day. Soon you will have copious discharge of urine and all problems connected with the urinary tract shall vanish in a week's time. Continue drinking raw milk and water mixture at least twice a day also.

□□

HOME REMEDIES

Some of the simple but useful home remedies are given below :

☐ For malaria fever 5-7 leaves mixed with powdered black pepper may be taken.

☐ 10 grams of tulsi juice mixed with 10 grams of Ginger juice removes pain in joints.

☐ Tulsi seed mixed with curd or honey stops vomiting in children.

☐ Black tulsi juice mixed with powdered black pepper mixed with oil (Ghee) removes gastric troubles.

☐ 25 grams of tulsi juice with 2 grams of black salt if taken 4 days destroys worms.

☐ Black tulsi (5 grams-25grams) mixed in honey cures asthmatic complaints.

☐ Black tulsi water mixed with Vinegar (same amount) mixed with butter is beneficial for Eczema conditions.

☐ Tulsi leaves heated in water used as drugs cures ear ache.

☐ For sore throat gargling with 10 grams of black tulsi boiled in 1/2 lit. water helps.

☐ Black tulsi leaves mixed with 7 almonds and 4 cardamoms (powdered) are good for indigestion.

☐ Black tulsi leaves mixed with honey (same amount) applied to the eyes, cures blur redness.

☐ Rub black tulsi juice (few drops) on the hands and feet of a person who has fainted.

- For excessive spit in the mouth black leaves should be chewed.

- The juice of tulsi leaves can be used to bring down fever. Extract of tulsi leaves in fresh water should be given every 2 to 3 hours. In between one can keep giving sips of cold water.

- In children, it is every effective in bringing down the high temperature. tulsi is an important constituent of many Ayurvedic cough syrups and expectorants. It helps to mobilize mucus in bronchitis and asthma. Chewing tulsi leaves relieves cold and flue.

- Power of seed of tulsi when taken with water gives great results in menstrual disorder.

- Root of tulsi is powdered and kept overnight in water, if taken daily early morning proves to be very beneficial in diabetes.

- Tulsi juice drops are very effective in earache.

- Tulsi juice when mixed with ginger juice is very effective in abdominal disorder in children.

- Powder of tulsi leaves added with saunth (dried ginger) and sugar when taken with hot water is a famous remedy for fever.

- Tulsi seeds processed in castor oil is very effective remedy for hair lice problem.

- It is said that if one tulsi leaf if swallowed daily, that person never suffers from cancer.

- Tulsi leaves boiled in water can be taken to cure sore throat. This water is also an ideal medium for gargle.

- Decoction of tulsi leaves, honey and ginger is an effective remedy for bronchitis, asthma and influenza.

- Tulsi leaves, besides being added to tea for taste, can also help in preventing feverishness. In acute fever, a decoction of tulsi leaves boiled with powdered cardamom, sugar and milk can lower and control the temperature.

- Basil is useful in reducing blood cholesterol as well as purification of blood.

- The leaves are good for nerves and to sharpen memory. Basil leaves are regarded as an adaptogen, anti-stress agent. Twelve basil leaves can be chewed twice a day to prevent stress. Chewing of basil leaves also cures ulcers and infections in mouth.

- Juice of basil leaves and honey taken regularly for six months can be useful in expelling renal stones.

- Tulsi is known for its antiseptic property to destroy bacteria and insects. A teaspoon of tulsi leaves juice can be taken at an interval of few hours in case of insect bite. Also fresh juice must be applied to the affected parts.

- Basil juice is an effective remedy for sore eyes and night blindness. Two drops of black basil juice should be put into the eyes daily at bedtime to cure this.

- Powder of dried tulsi leaves mixed with mustard oil can be used as toothpaste for maintaining dental health, countering bad breath and for massaging gums.

- Pounded leaves mixed with sandalwood paste can be applied on forehead to get relief from headache.

- A few drops of juice can be put in the ear to treat earache and dullness of hearing.

- The seeds of the plant are useful in treating diarrheoa, chronic dysentery and constipation.

- Tea made from leaves of tulsi controls nasal catarrh, cures body-ache and gives a refreshing feeling. Similarly, taking a few leaves mixed with a teaspoonful of ginger juice and honey immediately controls bouts of dry cough and removes any bronchial spasm.

- In chronic dysentery when a patient passes stool mixed with mucous, tulsi leaves offer great help. Taking them twice a day after mixing with a pinch of rock salt and half a teaspoon of roasted jeera powder in a bowl of curd acts as a good digestive. This treatment if continued for a week or 10 days also helps to dispel persistent wind and abdominal distension.

- Tusli seeds are known for their killer action on abdominal worms. Children suffering from roundworm infection can be safely given a quarter of a teaspoon of crushed tulsi seeds at bed time for at least three consecutive days.

- For chronic fever ancient Ayurvedic texts have extolled the use of tulsi leaves and its seeds. Regular use of its leaves during the season of viral fever acts as a good preventive medicine. References are also found where the juice of tulsi leaves is be applied for minor skin infections and also has a cure ear-ache.

- In a cup of tea 5 to 10 leaves can be added. The juice of its leaves can be taken up to 10 ml whereas the powder of its seeds can be taken in varying doses of 1 gram to 3 grams in a day.

- Basil has sedative and calming qualities. A basil sandwich, for example, will help to alleviate anxiety.

- Use basil as a gargle for clearing mouth infections—

pop a handful of basil in 250ml of boiling water and allow to stand for 5 minutes.

☐ Basil healing properties will help relieve the pain of tired and aching feet. Soak 2 cups of fresh basil leaves in 2 litres of water. Allow to cool and immerse feet for a good long soak. You can also crush the leaves and massage into your heels.

☐ It has been said, that a drop of basil juice from the leaves of the plant, has been very effective in the healing and relief of ear inflammation.

☐ Basil is also an antiseptic and antibacterial herb. Its healing properties can be used as a digestive aid to relieve nausea and an upset stomach.

☐ Basil is antispasmodic, so aids in the healing and relief of headaches and migraines, vertigo and even colic.

☐ As a culinary herb, basil is one of the most cleansing and helps with healing kidney and urinary problems.

☐ Basil provides a source of beta-carotene, estragole, eugenol, borneol and Vitamin C.

☐☐

HEALING POWER OF TULSI

The tulsi plant has many medicinal properties. The leaves are a nervine tonic and also sharpen memory. They promote the removal of the catarrhal matter and phlegm from the bronchial tube. The leaves strengthen the stomach and induce copious perspiration. The seed of the plant are mucilaginous.

Anxiety & Stress

Basil leaves are regarded as an adaptogen or anti-stress agent. Recent studies have shown that the leaves afford significant protection against stress. Even healthy persons can chew 12 leaves of basil, twice a day, to prevent stress. It purifies blood and helps prevent several common elements.

Common Cold & Fever

The leaves of basil are specific for many fevers. During the rainy season, when malaria and dengue fever are widely prevalent, tender leaves, boiled with tea, act as preventive against theses diseases. In case of acute fevers, a decoction of the leaves boiled with powdered cardamom in half a litre of water and mixed with sugar and milk brings down the temperature.

The juice of tulsi leaves can be used to bring down fever. Extract of tulsi leaves in fresh water should be given every 2 to 3 hours. In between one can keep giving sips of cold water. In children, it is every effective in bringing down the temperature.

Tulsi is an important constituent of many Ayurvedic

cough syrups and expectorants. It helps to mobilize mucus in bronchitis and asthma. Chewing tulsi leaves relieves cold and flu.

Sore Throat

Water boiled with basil leaves can be taken as drink in case of sore throat. This water can also be used as a gargle.

Respiratory Disorders

The herb is useful in the treatment of respiratory disorders. A decoction of the leaves, with honey and ginger is an effective remedy for bronchitis, asthma, influenza, cough and cold. A decoction of the leaves, cloves and common salt also gives immediate relief in case of influenza. They should be boiled in half a litre of water till only half the water is left and add then taken.

Kidney Stone

Basil has strengthening effect on the kidney. In case of renal stone the juice of basil leaves and honey, if taken regularly for 6 months it will expel them via urinary tract.

Heart Disorders

Basil has a beneficial effect in cardiac diseases and the weakness resulting from them. It reduces the level of blood cholesterol.

Children's Ailments

Common pediatric problems like cough, cold, fever, diarrhoea and vomiting respond favourably to the juice of basil leaves. If pustules of chicken pox delay their appearance, basil leaves taken with saffron will hasten them.

Mouth Infections

The leaves are quite effective for the ulcer and infections

in the mouth. A few leaves chewed will cure these conditions.

Insect Bites

The herb is a prophylactic or preventive and curative for insect stings or bites. A teaspoonful of the juice of the leaves is taken and a repeated after a few hours. Fresh juice must also be applied to the affected parts. A paste of fresh roots is also effective in case of bites of insects and leeches.

Skin Disorders

Applied locally, basil juice is beneficial in the treatment of ringworm and other skin diseases. It has also been tried successfully by some naturopaths in the treatment of leucoderma.

Eye Disorders

Basil juice is an effective remedy for sore eyes and night-blindness, which is generally caused by deficiency of vitamin A. Two drops of black basil juice should be put into the eyes daily at bedtimes.

Teeth Disorder

The herb is useful in teeth disorders. Its leaves, dried in the sun and powdered, can be used for brushing teeth. It can also be mixed with mustard oil to make a paste and used as toothpaste. This is very good for maintaining dental health, counter acting bad breath and for massaging the gums. It is also useful in pyorrhoea and other teeth disorders.

Headache

Basil makes a good medicine for headache. A decoction of the leaves can be given for this disorder. Pounded leaves mixed with sandalwood paste can also be applied on the forehead for getting relief from heat, headache.

TRADITIONAL USES

Today, basil is used mainly as a culinary herb. Its medicinal value is not as widely appreciated in the Western world.

Basil has been used to treat a variety of conditions, including the following: anxiety and tension, congestion, coughs, colds, colic, constipation, cuts and abrasions, diarrhoea, digestive disorders, dysentery, fevers, flatulence, headaches and migraines, insect bites and stings, menstrual cramps, muscle tension, nerve pain, nervousness, sinusitis, sore throats, tiredness and lethargy.

When inhaled in steam, it relieves nasal congestion.

Basil seeds contains mild antibiotic substances that, when used as a poultice, helps prevent skin infections and promotes the healing of minor skin wounds. Basil is also used in some skin ointments and promoted as a treatment for acne.

The tea is said to be relaxing, and, when taken in the evening, helps to promote sleep.

Chewing a couple of leaves before a meal helps to stimulate the appetite; and a tea taken after a meal promotes digestion by increasing the flow of gastric juices, while reducing gas and bloating.

In Chinese medicine, basil is used for disturbances in renal function, gum ulcers, and as a hemostyptic both before and after birth.

In Ayurvedic medicine, the juice is recommended for snake bites; as a general tonic; and for chills, coughs, rheumatoid arthritis, anorexia, skin problems, amenorrhea and dysmenorrhea, malaria, and earaches, but mainly used in the cases of fever. A classic recipe advocates mixing tulsi, black pepper, ginger, and honey to prevent infection and to control high fevers.

Since tulsi has the ability to lower blood pressure, it is thought to have an affinity for the heart, as well as helping the body to adapt to new demands and stresses.

Tulsi is used to reduce blood sugar levels as well as relieving fevers, bronchitis, asthma, stress, and canker sores. Research into its ability to reduce blood sugar levels has gone on for several decades, and is proving useful in some types of diabetes. Indian research has shown that the herb has anti-inflammatory, analgesic, and fever-reducing properties, as well as inhibiting sperm production.

Important

Tulsi has many extraordinary powers of healing and promoting health. tulsi is found to be endowed with purifying and antiseptic qualities. The efficacy of the remedies of skin diseases is greatly augmented if they are used in conjunction with tulsi. Here is a collection of a few such remedies:

❏ Equal amounts of 5 parts of the tulsi plant should be dried and powdered together. An extract of this powder has a purifying action on the blood. Regular use of this extract therefore prevents skin diseases.

❏ Application of a paste formed by grinding tulsi leaves with lemon juice is an effective treatment for ringworm.

❏ Continued ingestion of powdered tulsi roots and leaves with hot water is believed to cure all skin diseases.

❏ Boil tulsi leaves in mustard oil. When the leaves have turned completely black, take the oil off the flame and strain it. The application of this oil is beneficial in all skin diseases.

- Those suffering from scabies, ringworm or eczema should drink juice of tulsi leaves along with an external application on the affected parts.

- Dry tulsi leaves in the shade, add some alum, grind well and sieve through fine cloth. Store the powder in a clean dry glass bottle. This powder can be applied on any fresh cuts or wounds, and will promote quick healing.

- Application of tulsi juice on boils is beneficial and gives relief.

- Application of tulsi leaves ground in water from the river Ganga is believed to make skin eruptions subside in a very short time.

- Application of a paste of tulsi leaves and tender shoots of peepar (piper longum) on skin irritations resulting from plucking of hair provides relief.

- Pain due to burns is alleviated by applying equal quantities of tulsi juice and coconut oil mixed well.

- Rubbing with tulsi leaves over itching parts brings quick relief. Itching can also be soothed.

HOLY BASIL

Holy Basil is a lovely branched herb which grows only annually. Fitting it's name perfectly Hindus believe tulsi is a sacred plant. There are two types of tulsi. The first is characterized by a stronger scent and can be found near Suriname and is red and the other is green.

Holy basil should not be confused with the more commonly known basil, though they are cousins. Whereas basil is a leaf used to enliven cooking, Holy Basil is a clove like plant with a hairy appearance that has special significance in Hinduism and can very often be found growing wild in thick clusters around temples in India, which is more of a healing product than a culinary ingredient. Traditionally anyway, as there is a growing fashion to use Holy basil in cooking, particularly in the USA where chefs pioneered this new found usage.

But keeping with its more traditional uses, Holy basil is an ancient remedy with particular reverence in the Ayurvedic philosophy.

Ayurvedic prescribes Holy Basil as an agent of perspiration and as such it is recommended that the herb is taken having being brewed up into tea. It can then work in the body and sweat out feverish ailments such as the common cold and sore throats. When taken in this fashion it also has the effect of clearing blocked passageways and so is able to clear up bronchial disorders efficiently and safely.

The juice of the Holy Basil should also be applied to an afflicted area to combat skin disorders, particularly those such as ringworm and other similar complaints.

It also has particular qualities which seem able to relax

the body and give a feeling of the calm within a person when it is taken which enables Holy Basil to be used successfully as an anti-stress supplement and it is in this way it should be used for greater effect. Indeed it has been proven to be more successful in relieving stress then the more commonly known, better available and thus more frequently taken ginseng and it is said to be safer too with no known side effects.

Holy Basil is very much an emerging herb, certainly to the world outside of India and its' full benefits for a healthy lifestyle have yet to be fully explored, its de-stressing attributes are beyond doubt, but increasingly there is some evidence that it can be equally effective when prescribed as a painkiller, an anti-inflammatory medicine, a treatment for all bacterial, fungal and viral infections and perhaps what will become eventually its' most important usage, there is evidence that it can help lower and control blood sugar levels, which would not only make it a refreshing revitalizing tonic for all, but more specifically and significantly means that it could well end up being a common prescription in the treatment and alleviation of diabetes.

It should be said that these treatments are only at the trialing stage at the moment but there does seem to be good evidence and proper hope that Holy Basil can become a first-class treatment and a naturally healthy one to boot for all of these afflictions and complaints.

While Holy Basil has much spiritual significance, it does have many medicinal qualities.

Eye : When Holy Basil is crushed it produces a thick liquid which can be applied to the eyes for treatment of night blindness and inflammation.

Mouth : A powdered down version of Holy Basil can be used to treat sensitive teeth and gums. Adding water to the powder it can be used much like toothpaste. Also leaves can be chewed to promote the healing of mouth lesions and ulcers.

Bites: Any type of insect, spider, or outside critter bite can be treated using the liquid from crushed Holy Basil. Tulsi offers a prophylactic or anti-allergic properties which make sure that insects bites do not cause inflammation.

Distress: While in ancient times it was said that chewing Holy Basil leaves helped reduce stress related disorders it has been modernized. Today, Holy Basil tea and bath soaks are often the best remedy to relieve tension and stress daily.

High Cholesterol : Holy Basil much like the medication Lipitor which is used to lower cholesterol levels by several points. The great thing about Holy Basil is that it has none of the severe side effects of cholesterol medications like liver and kidney disease while still acting to lower cholesterol levels.

Upper Respiratory Infections: Holy Basil when combined with honey, salt, cloves, and lemon is a great resource for the relieving symptoms of cold. Flu, any upper respiratory infections, bronchitis, asthma, and cough. All ingredients are boiled down in one litre of water until half a liter remains and taken like tea.

Migraines : Holy Basil can be hammered into a paste which can then be applied to the head and neck to relieve the intense pain of migraines and severe headaches.

Skin Health : Holy Basil juice can always be applied to the skin to treat dry skin, rash, ring worm, and other infectious skin illnesses.

Digestive Tract : Holy Basil can stop all the nasty symptoms of food poisoning, stomach flu, and general children ailments including diarrheoa, and vomiting.

Kidney Stones : If Holy Basil juice is taking for 6 months it will allow for the easy expulsion of kidney stones via the urinary tract.

Obviously, Holy Basil is medicinal herb with many healing qualities. Just like any medication it should be taken under the supervision of a medical professional.

❑❑

NATURAL HEALING POWER

In India, tulsi is a revered native plant which has a place in all Hindu ceremonies and rituals. It is likely that it earned this place of honour due to its profound healing attributes which were understood and applied by the communities in which it grew. Tulsi (basil) and its healing power represent times past when people were deeply connected with nature and tapped into its treasures to find healing. In India, though the usage may have dwindled in medicinal prescriptions, tulsi still holds a place in many household courtyards, and is ceremoniously worshipped on special occasions as a symbol of prosperity and good health.

Traditionally, all parts of tulsi are used by itself or in combination with other herbs to alleviate a number of ailments and conditions. Tulsi's fragrant leaves and flowers in the form of tea, tincture, or decoction are an effective expectorant that alleviates symptoms of bronchitis, cough, diarrhea and skin condtions. Tulsi is also used as a prophylactic against epidemics like cholera, influenza, malaria and plague. Its uses as a mucilaginous and demulcent are well known, and the seeds are taken mixed in water or cow's milk for its

antioxidant and nourishing properties. This is generally used to boost low energy levels, cure ulcers, relieve vomiting and also as an analgesic when used topically to soothe insect bites and stings. Tulsi is also known to promote sexual stamina.

Tulsi is an energy-enhancing herb which is very similar in action and composition to other healing herbs such as ginseng and eleuthero. As a medicinal herb, tulsi improves resistance to stress, boosts immune function, normalizes blood pressure and blood sugar imbalance when eaten on a regular basis in the form of tea. It also protects and provides prophylactic effects against toxicity in the environment. Tulsi is rich in antioxidants, vitamins A, C and calcium.

The chemical constituents of tulsi contain a variety of biologically active compounds such as ursolic acid, apigenin and luteolin. The special attributes of tulsi (basil) are not easily understood at a microscopic level since it constitutes hundreds of healing substances known as phytochemicals. These phytochemicals have disease-fighting, antitoxin, and immunity-boosting qualities that promote vitality, energy, general health, natural immunity and longevity.

This medicinal herb acts as an antibacterial/ antiparasitic and therefore is widely used to treat infectious diseases. It is often used as an effective natural cure for upper respiratory tract infections like colds, coughs and bronchitis. It helps in preventing flatulence and constipation. Tulsi is an excellent expectorant and helps relieve symptoms of bronchitis and asthmatic conditions.

Tulsi acts as an anti-pyretic, smooth muscle relaxer, adaptogenic, immune system enhancer, and antioxidant. Cosmetically, it is known to have anti-aging properties, making the skin glow and appear youthful.

☐☐

TULSI POOJA

Tulsi is a consecrated plant that holds lot of importance for the traditional Hindus. In most of the Hindu homes, people worship Tulsi plant on a daily basis. Many people keep a plant of Tulsi in front of their house, since Tulsi has a lot of reverence for them. On the festive occasion of *Kartik Shukla Dwadashi* that usually falls two weeks after the celebration of Diwali, tulsi plants are adorned with varied artistic things made from sugarcane, flowers and mango leaves. After decorating Tulsi Vrindavana, people offer prayers to tulsi. Clay lamps are lit all around the tulsi plant. The event is usually celebrated as *Tulsi Vivah*, in which tulsi is married to Lord Vishnu.

Tulsi symbolizes devotion, love, responsibility, virtues and miseries of women. Tulsi is worshipped by females of all age groups. To perform tulsi pooja, one needs to take bath and get rid of all sorts of dirt, then be it physical or mental. People decorate the vessel or pot, in which tulsi is planted. Water is then offered to the plant. Kumkum is applied to one of the leaves. Some people tie a small piece of red cloth on its branch. Red flower is offered to the herbal plant tulsi. Clay lamps are lighted all around the plant and then aarti is performed to complete the pooja. On the completion of pooja, people usually eat a leaf of tulsi, with the belief that this act would enable them to take the Holy Spirit inside them.

The sacred plant, tulsi is regarded as the incarnation of the goddess Mahalakshmi. Tulsi represents duty, dedication, love, virtue and sorrow of all women. That is why this herb is usually worshipped by women of all age groups.

To begin tulsi pooja, one is required to take a bath. Decorate the pot where tulsi is grown. Offer water to the sacred plant. Apply kumkum on one of its leaf. A length of red cloth can be wrapped along the stem. Offer red flower to the sacred herb, tulsi. Offer fruits by placing them near the pot. Light the clay lamp and perform aarti to complete the tulsi pooja. People usually take a leaf of tulsi after the pooja and put it in their mouth. It is believed by committing such act; they are taking the spirit of goddess inside them.

❏❏

FREQUENTLY ASKED QUESTIONS

What are the different uses of the plant?

Tulsi is used both in medicine and worship. Greatly revered in the East as tested cure for a wide range of diseases, the leaves, wood and wood bark, roots, flowers and seeds all have highly medicinal properties. Tulsi has also found its way, some say because of the amazing healing potential, into the homes of many devout Hindus, for religious use. For some, in this way, the plant itself is worshiped and for others, the plant is used as a medium for worshiping.

What is the Ayurvedic constitution of tulsi?

The leaves of tulsi being the main portion of the plant used for medicine, all varieties are known throughout Ayurveda to be initially heating and drying, which makes tulsi ideal for eradicating ailments associated with the common cold. They also have a bitter quality to them and are easy to digest. Tulsi is classified as *rasayana*, a herb nourishing a person's growth and promoting long life; this is one reason why the sages prescribed tulsi as one of the eight indispensable things in Vedic worship. Tulsi is known as *tulam* which means incomparable, probably so-named for it's vast range of uses and benefits.

What does allopathic medicine say about tulsi?

To western medical practitioners, tulsi is regarded as an expectorant and a cure for malaria and other diseases, especially cold-induced ones like coughs, bronchitis, pneumonia, etc. The seeds can be used as a diuretic.

What about tulsi being taken by the aged, is this OK?

Tulsi is very useful for elderly people. It has repeatedly been documented to increase vitality and daily enthusiasm in the aged. There is no doubt that it greatly helps to improve memory as well as the overall quality of life.

Is tulsi suitable for everyone?

Generally speaking, tulsi is possibly the most beneficial substance, besides love, for the human race. This is further illustrated in the fact alone that the tulsi plant does not emit regular oxygen like most plants but rather produces ozone, helping to rebuild the earth's precious supply. The only type of people that should exercise caution, are those with a fiery constitution, as tulsi's properties are drying and heating. This is the case only for daily use by these people; a cup of tea every now and then, on a paced schedule actually will help to balance excess heat.

What is the best way to take tulsi tea?

Having a cup in the morning, before taking breakfast is most beneficial. Concluding the day with another cup, once the daily works are finished is also recommended.

Although taken first thing in the morning, tulsi can also be taken before, during or after food and throughout the day but most benefits are felt from having at least two cups a day. Tulsi can also be taken in a tincture form, or the dry leaves powdered and stuffed into capsules and swallowed.

What are the benefits of taking tulsi leaves?

Those who eat five leaves of tulsi daily remain protected from different types of diseases with enhanced memory power and intelligence. Old people do not experience weakness and remain protected from several chronic diseases.

Tulsi leaves are blood purifier. It enhances the beauty naturally. From medication purview it is not just a medicine but a super-medicine.

In Ayurveda it is considered as the destroyer of all the three *doshas*.

Taking juice of tulsi leaves with water on empty stomach in the morning increases the glow and memory power. It enhances digestive power as well. Tulsi juice immediately stops vomitting. Its juice is very helpful in malaria. It enhances the functioning of kidneys and is very helpful in case of acidity, piles, white spots on skin, obesity etc. Fever, cough and TB patients are benefited by taking three grams of tulsi every day. Tulsi juice with honey should be given for six months to patients suffering from stone problem. Cough, cold, fever, diarrhoea and vomiting etc. can be cured by tulsi. Its juice controls blood cholesterol level.

Ruchi Mehta's Cook Books Series

■ *Small Size* ■ *18 Colour Picture*

- Dal Curries & Pulao
- Ice Creams, Cakes & Puddings
- Aaloo Paneer Dishes
- Rajasthani Khaana

- Delicious Soups
- South Indian Food
- Party Cooking
- Tasty Snacks
- Microwave Cooking
- Chatpati Chaat
- Non Vegetarian Food
- Gujrati Dishes
- Vegetarian Chinese Foods
- Non Vegetarian Chinese Foods
- Zero Oil Cooking

- Pickles Chutenies & Murabbe
- Vegetarian Cook Book
- Punjabi Khaana
- Breakfast Specialists
- Laziz Mughalai Khaana

MANOJ PUBLICATIONS
761, Main Road Burari, Delhi-110084.